YOUR KNOWLEDGE HAS VALUE

- We will publish your bachelor's and master's thesis, essays and papers

- Your own eBook and book - sold worldwide in all relevant shops

- Earn money with each sale

Upload your text at www.GRIN.com
and publish for free

Bibliographic information published by the German National Library:

The German National Library lists this publication in the National Bibliography; detailed bibliographic data are available on the Internet at http://dnb.dnb.de .

Imprint:

Copyright © 2017 GRIN Verlag
Print and binding: Books on Demand GmbH, Norderstedt Germany
ISBN: 9783668887930

This book at GRIN:

https://www.grin.com/document/456368

Christoph Burmeister

The Effects of 9/11 on American Immigration Culture and Laws

How are the Taken Measures to be Assessed?

GRIN Verlag

GRIN - Your knowledge has value

Since its foundation in 1998, GRIN has specialized in publishing academic texts by students, college teachers and other academics as e-book and printed book. The website www.grin.com is an ideal platform for presenting term papers, final papers, scientific essays, dissertations and specialist books.

Visit us on the internet:

http://www.grin.com/

http://www.facebook.com/grincom

http://www.twitter.com/grin_com

Europagymnasium Kerpen

Research paper of

The effects of 9/11 on American immigration culture and laws

How are the taken measures to be assessed?

Christoph Burmeister

Table of contents

1. Introduction

In the summer holidays 2009 my parents and I arrived at the airport at 9 am. The day was a special one for me because it was going to be my first flight and I have always been interested in these big machines that fly at the sky without any contact to the ground. Because of that I wanted to see everything of an aircraft. How does it work? How is it possible to travel from one place to an other in such a little time? As I entered the aircraft it was overwhelming for me and I wanted to have a look at the cockpit because actually in there the whole airplane is controlled by the pilots. Which belongs to the question "How does the whole thing work?" again. So my parents asked the stewards for a short look in. But they answered that this would not be possible because of security reasons.

And exactly from the time when they gave this reply I was asking myself several times why there are these high security standards. Over the years I have slowly understood the reasons for the whole security because my father told me about September the 11th, 2001, when I became a bit older, so I was able to understand the relations between it. Kicking that up a notch in the preparations of my research paper the citizens of the United States came into my mind. I had already learnt a bit of the mixed culture because of the many immigrants who came to America and I wanted to know if there are any relations, too. Is the culture and the type of people affected by the new security standards after 9/11? Or were there no changes and the culture remains like it was all the years before? Information concerning this two subjects pre-9/11 and post-9/11 I am going to collect in the first big part of the research paper.

Out of the security and culture my topic was developed. I can imagine that many points out of these two subjects relate together. In addition to that there will be good possibilities to connect them and uncover the relations. This will be a good chance to compare security and immigration culture together and discuss the taken measures and changes by considering my own opinion in the second part under the question: "How are the taken measures to be assessed?"

At the end I hope I will be able to inform the people with my knowledge because only some know about the attacks in detail. Unfortunately this was a day that changed the entire world with its new type of terrorism and it is important for everyone to be well informed about how to deal with the issue of terror attacks.

2. Pre-9/11 Immigration policy

Immigration has always been a big topic in the United States. Many people from the whole world were searching for a new home and a better future. First I will have a look at the immigration and the resulting culture in course of the industrialization because of some big changes in these topics.

Before the industrialization there were almost immigrants "exclusively from the countries of northern and western Europe" [1]. These immigrants brought their families with them "seeking a permanent home in the New World" [2]. Most of them accepted jobs in the agriculture and after a few months they were well integrated with the population because of working in teams in their jobs. Therefore they were often mingled freely with the American population. This model of immigration had always been practised in America and it proved its worth; the people tried to integrate to the culture and they adopted the daily grind of the American inhabitants very fast. This kind of immigrant was part of the ʻoldʼ immigration model.

In the course of industrialization immigrants from southern and eastern Europe came to America which developed the ʻnewʼ immigration model. "This "new" immigration had consisted, it declared, largely of unskilled male laborers, a large proportion of whom had come to the United States not as permanent settlers" [3]. On that way there have developed the first transients who wanted to work in the USA at one place for a particular time and then journey on to an other place. "Die amerikanische Industrie brauchte Arbeitskräfte" [4] that is why many of the ʻnewʼ immigrants "had flocked to the industrial centers of the East and Middle West" [5]. The assimilation with them had been emerged as a very slow one because in the factories immigrants were working separated from the American workers. This is the reason why there were not many duties that had to be solved in a team, so they could not practise to speak English at work where they spent most of their time.

---

[1] Maldwyn Allen Jones (1992): p.152

[2] Maldwyn Allen Jones (1992a): p.152

[3] Maldwyn Allen Jones (1992b): p.152

[4] Peter Lösche (1999): p.88

[5] Maldwyn Allen Jones (1992c): p.152

At this time the United States recorded a very high immigration rate from all around the world. Until the beginning of the 20th century the immigrants were welcomed in America because of the lack of native workers in the country [6]. However some day the capacity of work was exhausted, too, and the government started to curb the immigration rate by declaring bans on immigrants especially for Asian countries. In addition to that it was stipulated that every immigrant needed to be literate or at least one member had to be if there was a family coming to America. But these measures actually did not serve their purpose to stop the high influx of immigration [7]. Because of that the laws were tightened again in the Immigration Acts of 1921 and 1924. In for the present last Act of 1924 was "restricted the number of any nationality entering the U.S. to 2 (accentuation by the author) percent of the foreign-born persons of that nationality who were residents of the country in 1910." [8] They had success and could curtail the wave of immigration.

Also Border Patrol became important at this time. After the numerical limitations of the immigrants, many people who wanted to immigrate to America unconditionally tried to get in illegally. Especially the Mexican immigrants got a problem at this time because they were never included to an Immigration Act so there were not any limitations for them [9]. Besides this Mexican wave of undocumented immigration has never been possible to stop until today. Because of this illegal immigration the American government started to support their Border Patrol to guard the country against these immigrants which became the major task of the organisation. The years after the Immigration Act of 1924 they got increased to 450 officers. The little institution grew up in the following years always supported by the government with new equipment, more officers and actually things that belongs to it [10]. All in all the borders of the United States were well protected but the security was not as special as it would be silhouetted against other border securities in other countries, what is going to be an important fact in the sequel of the research paper.

---

[6] Cf. Christian Kube (2009): p. 21

[7] Armando Navarro (2009): p. 30

[8] Armando Navarro (2009a): p. 30

[9] Cf. Christian Kube (2009a): p. 21

[10] *Border Patrol History*; 6.10.2017 on Official website of the Department of Homeland Security

From the Border Security I will have a closer look at the reasons why the American citizens did not have a problem with the polymorphic conflicts of assimilation of the immigrants from the other countries again. There was a specific cause I am going to introduce you in in the following.

The book *The Epic of America*, written by James Truslow Adams, was the starting point of the so called "American Dream" in 1931. Many of the American inhabitants had already had the view of a multicultural country on their United States before but this was actually the first phrase that described this imagination. A reason for the popularity of the phrase is that "*The Epic of America* was the best-selling non-fiction work right through" [11].

The actual meaning of the American Dream which is traditionally under lock and key in the American population and culture is also declared in *The Epic of America*:

> that American dream of a better, richer and happier life for all our citizens of every rank which is the greatest contribution we have as yet made to the thought and welfare of the world. That dream or hope has been present from the start. Ever since we became an independent nation, each generation has seen an uprising of the ordinary Americans to save that dream from the forces which appeared to be overwhelming and dispelling it. (p. 20)

So all in all this dream wants to enable every single citizen to live its own satisfying life and achieve their aims without any matter of ranking in society. Everybody deserves it by working hard for it. This applies to the immigrants from different countries, too.

In addition to that the following two metaphorical theories are more suitable for the view of immigrants and their social reputation but relate to the American Dream again. The reason for these two theories is the view of the American citizens on their country. They consider it as a new "Nation of Immigrants" [12] which should express their openness in this point. Out of this view there has developed the following two theories.

The first metaphorical description of the American society is the *Melting Pot*, which arises from Roman von Jean de Crèvecoeur. He asked himself *What is an American?* and answered it in his book *Letters from an American Farmer*: "*In the United States of America* (accentuation by the author) individuals of all nations are melted into a new race of actual

---

[11] James Truslow Adams (1931 -> reissue from 2012): p.4

[12] Susan F. Martin (2011): p. 183

men[...]"[13]. In this statement the first part of the metaphor *melted* is already existing but the actual phrase got popular more than one hundred years later as a same titled play went through the USA. Many citizens of the United States supported the term because they considered it as a good description that suited their country. The idea of the *Melting Pot* is that every single immigrant who comes from all around the world gives up his or her identity of the old homeland. The culture and language belongs to that. Immigrants have to adapt themselves in this points to be accepted in the society of the United States. So actually the immigrants are melted in a pot everyone is the same and a member of the similar nationality in [14]. There are no problems for immigrants to assimilate to the daily grind. In addition to that a picture has developed out of these considerations. You can see the pot which is called "Citizenship" and all the immigrants are put in. One person who represents the stature of liberty stirs in this pot with a big spoon you can find the following sign on: "equal rights" (cf. fig 1) . All in all in the picture of the *Melting Pot* the immigrants become a part of the American society by completely giving up their identity to be treated equally in the country.

The second metaphor to describe the American society is the *Salad Bowl*, which got popular in the seventies and eighties, so it is a much newer version of the description compared to the *Melting Pot*. If you have a look at a usual salad bowl "each ingredient in a tossed salad retains its own color, texture, taste *and* (accentuation by the author) individual identity." [15] Translating this into the society of the United States every citizen - does not matter if immigrant or not - can keep his own identity without getting bared from the society. It is the ideology of the *Salad Bowl* that the identities are mixed but not blended together in the society so that there is going to arise a multicultural and classless one [16]. Many people considered this phrase as a good alternative to look at their countries` immigration culture, especially because it is almost impossible to forget your own identity like it is supposed to be in the *Melting Pot*.

---

[13] J. Hector St. John de Crèvecoeur (1782 -> reissue from 1997): p. 44

[14] Cf. www.lmg.pf.bw.schule.de/faecher/englisch/.../files/meltingbowl.doc -> *Metaphors of American society*

[15] David Ng (1996): p.205

[16] Cf. Eunjoo Mary Kim (2010): p. 105

3. Post-9/11 Immigration policy

The September 11, 2001, was a day that not only changed the United States of America. Three attacks that shocked the world within one day. Attacks that were unknown to the world because of the initiation of a terrorist organization called *Al-Qaeda*. An organization that came from close to scratch and directly attacked the superpower USA to achieve their ideologies. 2973 lives were lost at this day because of the attacks. A few days after the dramatic attacks president Bush proclaimed the *War on Terror* against the *Al-Qaeda* organization [17]. In the following I am going to clarify the measures which has been taken from the government and the actual situation in the society and culture.

"The 9/11 hijackers entered the country with legally issued visas - a fact that immediately linked immigration with terrorism and national security" [18]. The national security will be the main topic in the following measures that were taken by the government. In this category you can see the most dramatic changes and you can refer these measures to the terror attacks of 9/11.

The first reaction of the government was to pass the Aviation and Transportation Security Act on November 19, 2001, about two months after the attacks. Out of this Act the *Transportation Security Administration (TSA)* was emerged and its duties were and are to cater for the necessary security of the aviation. This security task is one of the most important duty they are responsible for. And everything caused only by the events of September the 11th. You can see this importance of the aviation security by having a look at the components of the budget of the Transportation Security Administration. 84% of it is spent to protect the aviation of the country so it falls into place that this must be the most important issue of this agency. 2003 parts of *TSA* got part of the Department of Homeland Security [19]. This participation effected a higher budget of the government at the same time to reach their aims and improve the agency's work.

---

[17] Cf. Tom Lansford, Robert P. Watson, Jack Covarrubias (2009): p. 57

[18] Michelle Mittelstadt, Burke Speaker, Doris Meissner, Muzaffar Chishti (2011): p.1

[19] Cf. Jane Bullock, George Haddow, Damon P. Coppola (2009): p. 235

The government also started to held hearings with already arrested Muslims in the United States to get to know the religion that has attacked the whole country and hurt everyone with the happenings in such a hard way [20]. The religion was nearly unknown to the Americans so that they thought about them doubtfully. Especially the American citizens started hating the Muslims and were willing to defend their fatherland [21] by taking revenge on the initiators of the whole situation. "The association of Islam with the most deadly terrorist attacks in the U.S. history intensified pre-existing prejudices against the faith and its followers [...]" [22] This quotation actually describes the view of the American citizens well. The majority of the population in the United States held the Muslims responsible for the attacks so it must be really hard for them to integrate to America after September the 11th. Therefore nobody will have any trust in them so they do not have any social basis for living there.

An other measure is the *Airport Passenger Screening* which is practised before a flight. The aim is to detect items that are prohibited to take with you on a flight. For example items which can be used as a weapon like knives or disabling chemicals to hurt people, overcome the crew to skyjack and so on. There are two general steps that compose the screening at the airports. First the passengers get checked by a Transportation security officer (TSO) by only patting the passenger down without any additives. They are responsible for those items the passengers maybe want to smuggle beyond the actual checkpoint of security. The second thing to check the passengers is the technology stuff with the X-ray machines, walk-through metal detectors, explosive trace detection equipment and handheld metal detectors so that the passengers´ baggage is also controlled and the things the TSO has lost sight of can be found, too [23]. The TSA is especially founded to take the responsibility for the security after 9/11. Before the attacks "the aircraft operator was mainly responsible for passenger and baggage screening at major airports." [24] Furthermore the items you can take with you on a flight are restricted today. 2008 the International Civil Aviation Organization (ICAO) released a list of items that will be prohibited in the aircrafts. For example it is not allowed to take more than

---

[20] Cf. Julie Farnam (2005): p. 79

[21] Cf. Avi Primor (2004): p. 15

[22] Lori Peek (2011): p. 63

[23] Cf. Gregory D. Kutz (2007): p. 4-5

[24] Paul Seidenstat, Francis X. Splane (2009): p. 77

100 millilitres in one package in your hand baggage anymore as well as sharp objects which can cause injuries to other passengers [25]. All these items would never be a problem pre-9/11.

Nowadays Donald Trump became president of the United States of America and for many people it is dubious how he will construct the immigration policy in the future. In an article written by him he declared a few aims concerning this topic. Firstly he wants to support the screening process like it was already practised in the past and amplify the data acquisition of the immigrants and refugees. In addition to that he is willing to improve the United States Refugee Admissions Program which indicates that refugees are welcomed in the USA and provides protection all around the world for these refugees who come to America. Furthermore the screening of the immigrants before entering the country is going to be tightened. Especially the refugees and immigrants from the countries that are recommended as a heightened risk to the American security (Iran, Libya, Somalia, Sudan, Syria and Yemen) should be screened and controlled copiously [26].

4. Discussion of the measures

Now I have collected the necessary information for the following text where I am going to discuss the taken measures of the government and introduce my own opinion into this discussion.

The first measure that has also changed the biggest part in the type of immigrants and culture were the hearings of the Muslims by the government - antedated the fact that the terrorist attacks were actually organized by the Muslim organization *Al-Qaeda*.

On the one hand it was positive because the nation got to know the religion that has attacked the country in this intensive way. Before the attacks the citizens were uncertain how to think about the religion Islam which represents the *Al-Qaeda* organization. This could be a chance to enlighten everyone who was living in the dubiety after the attacks and expand their horizon.

---

[25] Cf. Ronald I C Bartsch (2012): p. 238

[26] Cf. Donald J. Trump (2017): Executive Order Protecting The Nation From Foreign Terrorist Entry Into The United States (Website)

On the other hand the hearing did not redound to equal treatment and produced hate of the American citizens concerning the Muslim immigrants in the USA. "Anti-Muslim hate crimes are still five times more common today than before 9/11." [27] The criminal treatment against the Muslims has gained since September the 11th intensively which shows the influence of the hearings again. Comparing the situation with pre-9/11 an other negative point is striking. The American dream is broken on that score and metaphors like *Melting Pot* or *Salad Bowl* does not apply for the Muslims anymore. Ideas of an equal living together is not possible today because of the prejudices the American population have. Therefore it is difficult to assimilate for the Muslims.

I think all in all the hearings are not the only reason why the Muslims are not well accepted in the society anymore but they have accounted for it. It is not fair to treat the Muslims like they are treated today because actually they are not able to change their identity. They have been Muslim for their whole life and only because of some Muslims who initiated the attacks every other Muslim get generalized by the state by conducting theses hearings. Because of this degradation the citizens also started deprecating them so that it is not possible for Muslims to live socially integrated. This behaviour I would actually never have expected from the American population because there were many examples in the past where the immigration was difficult but they always could manage to assimilate the immigrants at this time well (for example in the industrialization). That are the reasons why I think that this hearings were the wrong way to get to know the religion and tell the population about the birds and the bees.

The second measure I am going to have a look at is the *Airport Passenger Screening* which should improve the security at travelling and also at the borders.

The strongest argument the advocates make a case for the screening process is that security was highly improved by the new security standards after September the 11th. There are not any possibilities to take prohibited items on flights anymore or to enter the country as an immigrant illegally thanks to the efficient monitoring.

On the other hand the painstaking screening often results in long waiting times. Especially when many passengers are visiting the airport and there are not enough screening modules for this moment the passengers are obliged to wait for their checking a long time. Many

---

[27] Cari Lee Skogberg Eastman (2017): p. 20

passengers who had made use of short-haul flights in the past already changed their mobility device which damages the airline companies because of lost customers. Furthermore the space at the airport is constrained by the whole security devices that are necessary for checking. The airport could be much more profitable without the whole security stuff - for example with more gates in areas the checking takes place. In addition to that money plays a big role. First you have the asset costs of the whole equipment. These high-tech machines are really expensive and the airport needs many of them because of the many passengers who want to travel by the aircrafts. Working employees want to be paid, too, so this is money that has to be spend every month for the salaries. Besides the screening shows everything what determine in the suit cases. Screeners who use the handheld metal detectors sometimes also have to check aggravating points at the body to make sure that there are no illegal items carried along. Especially women have often complained about that because they felt taking a hand in their privacy [28].

I would say that the security measures at the airports in general are elaborate well in many points. You need to bring up much effort and especially money to achieve only creating the whole security area at the airport and this is really disadvantageous. But by surveying the topic I think this effort really pays off because every passenger can feel secured at their flights. The whole issue is an investment for the future because if the machines are bought for the first time there are only current costs with the employees what occurs in every field of work. Even Donald Trump whose opinion often leans against the refugees and immigrants is willing to improve the screening in the future. Because the screening takes a long time some passengers replace the airlines with travelling by train or something else because of the lost time they spend on the airport. But as a result I think in this case it is more important to give every passenger a feeling of being secured instead of saving money and time. That is why I think this measure is reconsidered well and why I believe in the *Airport Passenger Screening* in the future, too.

In addition to that I have carved out the *Transportation Security Administration* as a measure that was taken. This agency is actually responsible for all the new security standards after 9/11 and cooperates with the *Department of Homeland Security*.

---

[28] Cf. Bartholomew Elias (2009): p. 198

The TSA was founded after 9/11 as a separated agency which already results in a big advantage for the whole security in the aviation sector. The separation procures a much better organization and concentration on the actual task - the security. Seemingly before 9/11 this was a problem in the United States because of this absence of the components the TSA is now able to raise. Maybe if this agency had already existed before September the 11th, it would have been possible to prevent the dramatic happenings on that day. There has also arose many employments by founding such a big new agency like the TSA which always strengthen a country.

All in all I think the American government has taken their measures by involving the fear and anger of their citizens at the happenings on 9/11 and excluding the people from other countries; especially the Muslim countries. On the one hand the measures were aimed at the American citizens who first lived a life in dubiety and did not know how to behave shortly after the attacks. We had the changes in the security. Many investments in this sector should give the citizens the feeling of being secured again. Especially these measures were taken there because if the aviation had already been protected as good as today the whole event of 9/11 would not have been that possible to conduct. The measures in this topic were a good representation of the population's opinion because they were alienated to trust in the aviation after September the 11th and with the government's changes the citizens get this trust back. Every measure in the field of security was a benefit that brings the inhabitants back to trust their country again. On the other hand there is one measure that was not taken well. The hearings actually wanted to clear the difficult situation of the initiators and the corresponding religion up. This elucidation was successful so that nowadays everyone knows about Al-Qaeda and its religion Islam but I think it was executed in a wrong way. Because today the people who are part of the Islam are excluded from the American population because of many prejudices against them that has been elicited by the hearings. This makes it impossible to live in American well immigrated for a Muslim person although he or she actually comes to the United States in peace. So the measures were well taken by the government excluding the hearings of the Muslim detainees.

5. Conclusion

I started my research paper by contemplating the immigration history before the terrorist attacks on September the 11th, 2001. At this time America and especially the citizens looked at the immigrants in a very different light as today. The population got used to immigration waves from foreign countries from all around the world and that the United States was not a state that exclusively is consisted of native Americans. Many conceptions like the American dream or metaphorical ideas like the Melting Pot or Salad Bowl held the citizens of barring immigrants from the society. Even difficult assimilation times like the industrialization did not pose a challenge for them. They were always willing to affiliate the 'new' members in their society. 9/11 was a change in the immigration that has never been so dramatic before. The culture was destroyed and not a one big society anymore where everyone is equally treated in. Citizens of the U.S. started looking at some immigrants doubtfully without any trust in them. This resulting distance between native Americans and immigrants redounds to a split population which destroys every view the United States was popular for in the past. More than 15 years are already passed by since the attacks and the citizens still keep away especially from the Muslim immigrants. So time is not a solution in this case to unite the society again. In the future the situation will not be simplified with the new president Donald Trump. His plan to build a wall between the American and Mexican border because of the continuing wave of illegal immigration from Mexico is maybe going to protect the country from these immigrants but the distances in the American society will be increased again. It will take much time until they are able to live with the immigrants together like it was in the past. The government tried to get the trust of the population back by combating the actual cause of the attacks of 9/11. What has been happened was such a new type of terrorism and the government first had to learn dealing with this issue. The security was improved with many new technologies and much money to spend in this sector. All in all the immigration culture today was influenced by September the 11th. Today especially Muslim immigrants are often suspended from the society because many native Americans call them to account the happenings of 9/11 in the organisation of Al-Qaeda. Mexican immigration is also going to be difficult in the future because of Donald Trump who constitute his approach with 9/11 again. I think 9/11 should not be a date in the future everyone can explain his thuggery against immigrants and foreigner with how Donald Trump tries to do. Everyone should be treated equally without any matter of his or her identity if the behaviour is corresponding.

6. Appendix

[Diese Abbildung wurde aus urheberrechtlichen Gründen von der Redaktion entfernt.]

Fig. 1: The Melting Pot

7. Bibliography

I. Books

Adams, James Truslow. *The Epic of America*. Boston: Little, Brown and Company, 1931 -> reissue from 2012

Bullock, Jane & Haddow, George and P. Coppola, *Damon. Introduction to Homeland Security: Principles of All-Hazards Response (Third edition)*. Burlington: Elsevier, 2009

Covarrubias, Jack & Lansford, Tom and P. Watson, Robert. *America's War on Terror, Second Edition*. Farnham: Ashgate Publishing, 2009

D. Kutz, Gregory. *Aviation Security: Vulnerabilities Exposed Through Covert Testing of TSA's Passenger Screening Process*. Washington, D.C.: United States Government Accountability Office, 2007

Elias, Bartholomew. *Airport and Aviation Security: U.S. Policy and Strategy in the Age of Global Terrorism*. CRC Press Taylor & Francis group: Boca Raton, 2009

Farnam, Julie. *U.S. Immigration Laws Under the Threat of Terrorism*. New York: Algora Publishing, 2005

I C Bartsch, Ronald. *International Aviation Law: A Practical Guide*. New York: Ashgate Publishing, 2012

Jones, Maldwyn Allen. *American Immigration*. Chicago: The University of Chicago Press, 1992

Kube, Christian. *Immigration und Arbeitskämpfe in den USA: US-Gewerkschaften und transnationale mexikanische Arbeiter; das Beispiel Kalifornien*. Potsdam: Universitätsverlag Potsdam, 2009

Lee Skogberg Eastman, Cari. *Immigration: Examining the Facts.* Santa Barbara: ABC-CLIO, 2017

Lösche, Peter. *Länderbericht USA: Geschichte, Politik, Wirtschaft, Gesellschaft, Kultur.* Frankfurt / New York: Campus Verlag, 1999

Martin, Susan F.. *A Nation of Immigrants.* Cambridge / New York: Cambridge University Press, 2011

Mary Kim, Eunjoo. *Preaching in an Age of Globalization.* Louisville, Kentucky: Westminster John Knox Press, 2010

Navarro, Armando. *The Immigration Crisis: Nativism, Armed Vigilantism, and the Rise of a Countervailing Movement.* Plymouth: AltaMira Press, 2009

Ng, David. *People on the Way: Asian North Americans Discovering Christ, Culture, and Community.* Valley Forge: Judson Pr, 1996

Peek, Lori. *Behind the Backlash: Muslim Americans After 9/11.* Philadelphia: Temple University Press, 2011

Primor, Avi. *Terror als Vorwand.* Düsseldorf: Droste Verlag GmbH, 2004

Seidenstat, Paul. and X. Splane, Francis. *Protecting Airline Passengers in the Age of Terrorism.* Santa Barbara: ABC-CLIO, 2009

St. John de Crèvecoeur, J. Hector. *Letters from an American Farmer.* Oxford / New York: Oxford University, 1782 -> reissue from 1997

II. Fact Sheet

Chishti, Muzaffar et al.. *Through the Prism of National Security: Major Immigration Policy and Program Changes in the Decade since 9/11*. Washington D.C.: Migration Policy Institute, 2011

III. Websites

"Metaphors of American society"
www.lmg.pf.bw.schule.de/faecher/englisch/.../files/meltingbowl.doc; 15.10.2017 (worksheet from the lessons)

"Border Patrol History". U.S. Customs and Border Protection, October 6, 2017, U.S. Department of Homeland Security, 24.10.17, https://www.cbp.gov/border-security/along-us-borders/history

Donald J. Trump. Executive Order Protecting The Nation From Foreign Terrorist Entry Into The United States, March 06, 2017, The White House, 28.10.2017, https://www.whitehouse.gov/the-press-office/2017/03/06/executive-order-protecting-nation-foreign-terrorist-entry-united-states

IV. Figure in Appendix

Figure 1: https://classracegender.files.wordpress.com/2014/02/melting_pot.jpg

YOUR KNOWLEDGE HAS VALUE

- We will publish your bachelor's and
  master's thesis, essays and papers

- Your own eBook and book -
  sold worldwide in all relevant shops

- Earn money with each sale

Upload your text at www.GRIN.com
and publish for free